Hampshire's Lost Railways

by
Marie Panter

Locomotive No. 109, 'Southampton', at Southampton Royal Pier, June 1894. This locomotive was built by Shanks in December 1876 and withdrawn from service in December 1913.

First published in the United Kingdom, 2005,
by Stenlake Publishing Ltd.
Telephone: 01290 551122
www.stenlake.co.uk
Printed by Cordfall Ltd., Glasgow, G21 2QA

ISBN 1 84033 362 6

The publishers regret that they cannot supply copies of any pictures featured in this book.

PICTURE ACKNOWLEDGEMENTS

The publishers wish to thank the following for contributing photographs to this book: John Alsop for the front and inside front covers, and pages 2–4, 7–10, 12, 13, 15–23, 25–43, 45–48 and the back cover; and Richard Casserley for pages 1, 5, 6, 11, 14, 24 and the inside back cover.

An 0-4-4T locomotive with the '1.30 p.m. special' at Longmoor Station on the Longmoor Military Railway.

INTRODUCTION

Railways were built in many parts of Britain during the 'Railway Mania' of the late 1830s and 1840s and Hampshire was no different, particularly as developers were keen to create links between London and the south coast and the Isle of Wight. One company predominated in Hampshire – the London & South Western Railway – which was responsible for the main line from London Waterloo to the West Country, which passes right through Hampshire, and many of the branch lines that ran around the country.

The railways in Hampshire ranged from small country branch lines such as the Salisbury & Dorset Junction Railway and the Hayling Island Branch line, to main lines such as the London to Southampton railway. As well as civilian railways, the county also had two standard gauge military railways which are now closed. There was also a narrow gauge railway located at RAF Calshot, but this too has long since closed. There was also over 25 miles of railways situated behind the walls of Portsmouth Docks.

Railways have undergone three phases since their initial development. By the 1920s there were 120 separate operating companies in Britain, but in 1923 these were grouped into four operating companies; in Hampshire this was the Southern Railway. The final phase occurred in 1948 when the entire network was nationalised under British Railways. Unfortunately, due to Dr Beeching's 'Reshaping Plan', many of the county's railways were closed.

The 'Calshot Express' at RAF Calshot.

Andover & Redbridge Railway

Passenger service withdrawn	7 September 1964
Distance	28 miles (Andover to Redbridge)
Company	Andover & Redbridge Railway (1858–63)/ London & South Western Railway (1863–1923)

Stations closed	*Date*
Andover Town	7 September 1964
Clatford	7 September 1964
Fullerton Junction*	7 September 1964
Stockbridge	7 September 1964
Horsebridge	7 September 1964
Mottisfont	7 September 1964

Andover Town Station.

* Originally named Fullerton Bridge; renamed as Fullerton on 1 October 1871. Closed on 1 June 1885 and a second station opened due south on the same date. Renamed as Fullerton Junction on 7 July 1929.

Clatford Station, 24 May 1957.

Following the route of the 1794 Andover to Redbridge canal, this line was promoted in 1858 as an independent railway, and after being sought by both the Great Western and the London & South Western railways – the latter gaining control – the line was opened throughout on 6 March 1865 as a single line, with crossing loops at the stations to enable trains to pass when necessary. It took passenger trains 90 minutes to complete the 28-mile journey.

Stockbridge Station, *c*.1911.

Fullerton Station (later Fullerton Junction) was moved a few hundred yards south of its original location with the arrival of the branch line from Hurstbourne in 1885. Travelling north east from Romsey, the line separated at Kimbridge Junction, running in one direction towards Salisbury and in the other to Andover Junction. There were four goods loops laid during 1943 in order to ease the congestion caused by wartime traffic. The two outer loops were taken out of service in 1948 and the remaining two loops were removed in 1952 after being used to store condemned locomotives.

Horsebridge Station.

Horsebridge Station.

Basingstoke & Alton Light Railway

Passenger service withdrawn	1 June 1936
Distance	12 miles (Basingstoke to Alton)
Company	London & South Western Railway (1844–1923)

Stations closed	*Date*
Cliddesden *	12 September 1932
Herriard *	12 September 1932
Bentworth & Lasham *	12 September 1932

Cliddesden Station, *c*.1909.

* Closed between 1 January 1917 and 18 August 1924.

Cliddesden Station.

Authorised in 1896, this light railway finally opened on 1 June 1901 – nearly 20 years after the first plans had been laid down. The railway was famous as the first to be constructed under the newly approved Light Railway Act. This meant that only lighter than normal trains could run, with a restricted speed limit of 25 mph imposed on the line. From end to end the total journey time was 45 minutes. The line was single throughout, except for a few yards approaching Butts Junction when the line widened into two. Most of the stations were located some distance from the towns they served and Herriard was the only one to have two platforms.

The 7.30 a.m. train from Alton to Basingstoke at Cliddesden, 13 June 1931.

The railway closed during the First World War and the track between Thorncroft's Works and Lord Mayor Trelsar's Hospital was lifted and exported to France during 1917. Because of high public demand the tracks were relaid after the war, although not until August 1924.

Herriard Station, *c*.1911.

The reopened railway never made any commercial sense, as the distance between Basingstoke and Alton was too short and with all the stops the journey took too long. As a result, passenger services were withdrawn on 12 September 1932. Goods services continued for a while between Basingstoke and Bentworth & Lasham, but all the stations were closed on 1 June 1936. There was one final use for the railway – in 1937 the line was used during the filming of *Oh Mr Porter*, with Cliddesden Station playing the part of the fictional Buggleskelly.

Bentworth & Lasham Station, *c*.1908.

Bentley & Bordon Light Railway

Passenger service withdrawn	4 April 1966	*Stations closed*	*Date*
Distance	5 miles (Bentley to Bordon Camp)	Kingsley Halt	16 September 1957
Company	London & South Western Railway (1902–23)	Bordon	16 September 1957

The locomotive 'Earl Roberts' at Bordon Station with the 11.15 a.m. to Longmoor, 17 May 1934.

Bentley Station opened in July 1857, although the branch to Bordon was not authorised until 1902. Bordon Station opened on 11 December 1905, with Kingsley Halt following on 7 March 1906. The branch closed to passengers in 1957, although Bentley is still in use as part of the Alton to Waterloo service. The branch was built to serve Bordon Camp and the surrounding military towns. Bordon was also the interchange point for the north terminus of the Longmoor Military Railway, which had a station adjacent to the London & South Western Railway station.

Bishops Waltham Branch

Passenger service withdrawn	2 January 1933
Distance	4 miles (Botley to Bishops Waltham)
Company	Bishops Waltham Railway (1862–63)/ London & South Western Railway (1863–1923)

Stations closed	*Date*
Botley	2 January 1933
Durley Halt	2 January 1933
Bishops Waltham	2 January 1933

Bishops Waltham Station.

Bishops Waltham Station, *c*.1905.

Authorised on 17 July 1862 and opened on 1 June the following year, the Bishops Waltham Railway ran for 4 miles from its junction with the main line at Botley and followed the course of the River Hamble. Initially, there were only two stations on the line but Durley Halt was opened on 23 December 1909, located 1.5 miles from Botley and 2.5 miles from Bishops Waltham. Due to financial difficulties the Bishops Waltham Railway Company were unable to complete the terminus station until two years after opening. The new station replaced a temporary one and was built by the local brickworks in such a fashion that the quality of their products was displayed. The London & South Western Railway took control in 1881, even though they had been working the line for many years previous. Initial service was six trains in each direction, with three on Sundays. In early 1931 the Sunday services were axed due to a decline in passenger numbers and the engine sheds were also closed. These measures were insufficient to keep the line open and it was closed to passenger services on 2 January 1933. Goods traffic continued, at first twice daily, reduced to daily, and finally to two or three times per week, until final closure of the line on 27 April 1962. After closure an attempt was made by Hampshire Narrow Gauge Railway Society to use part of the trackbed for a 2-foot gauge line, but the attempt failed.

Bishopstoke to Gosport

Passenger service withdrawn	6 June 1953
Distance	Unknown
Company	London & South Western Railway

Stations closed	*Date*
Fort Brockhurst *	8 June 1953
Gosport **	8 June 1953
Clarence Yard ***	1 February 1901

Fort Brockhurst Station.

* Originally known as Brockhurst until 22 November 1893.
** Closed between 3 December 1841 and 7 February 1842.

*** Also known as Gosport Royal Victoria; closed after the death of Queen Victoria when Osborne House was presented to the public.

0-4-2 class A12 locomotive, No. 604, at Gosport Station, 1931.

The branch line to Gosport was authorised in 1839 and opened on 29 November 1841, but was closed four days later due to a landslip north of Fareham. The line was eventually reopened on 7 February 1842. Prior to the arrival of the railway in Portsmouth, Gosport provided the service to London for the local community and passengers from Portsmouth had to cross to Gosport by ferry. Gosport Station was positioned two and a half miles from the town as the military authorities initially would not give permission to allow the towns fortifications to be breached. However, for Her Majesty's convenience, permission was granted in 1844 and the railway extended 500 metres into Clarence Yard, where a station was erected for exclusive use by Queen Victoria who frequented Gosport on route to Osborne House on the Isle of Wight.

A detachment of Royal Scots Fusiliers leaving Gosport Station.

Due to the opening of Portsmouth Station in 1847 passenger services to and from Gosport suffered a decline and, although the line saw a lot of activity during the First World War, the railway was reduced to a single line in 1934. Services further declined and the line eventually closed to passengers in 1953, although freight services survived until 1969.

Didcot, Newbury & Southampton Junction Railway *

Passenger service withdrawn	7 March 1960
Distance	44 miles
	(Didcot to Winchester via Newbury and Highclere)
Company	Didcot, Newbury & Southampton Railway (1885–23)/ Great Western Railway (1923–48)

Stations closed	*Date*
Woodhay **	7 March 1960
Highclere **	7 March 1960
Burghclere **	7 March 1960
Litchfield ***	7 March 1960
Whitchurch Town ****	7 March 1960
Sutton Scotney **	7 March 1960
Worthy Down Halt *****	7 March 1960
King's Worthy **	7 March 1960
Winchester Chesil †	7 March 1960

Highclere Station, *c*.1910.

* The closed station that was on this line in Oxfordshire was Upton & Blewbury. Closed stations in Berkshire were Churn, Compton, Hampstead Norris, Pinewood Halt and Hermitage.

** Closed between 4 August 1942 and 8 March 1943.

*** Renamed as Litchfield (Hants) on 7 June 1909; closed between 4 August 1942 and 8 March 1943; reverted to original name on 13 June 1955.

**** Originally known as Whitchurch; renamed as Whitchurch (Hants) on 1 July 1924; closed between 4 August 1942 and 8 March 1943; renamed as Whitchurch Town on 26 September 1949.

***** Originally named Worthy Down Platform; closed between 4 August 1942 and 8 March 1943; renamed on 18 June 1951.

† Originally known as Winchester Cheesehill; closed between 4 August 1942 and 8 March 1943; renamed on 26 September 1949; closed between 7 March and 18 June 1960 and 10 September 1960 and 17 June 1961; finally closed on 9 September 1961.

Burghclere Station.

In 1882 a single track railway opened from Didcot, Oxfordshire, to Newbury in Berkshire. In 1885 the line was extended to Winchester, again as a single track. In 1891 a junction was created with the London & South Western Railway at Shawford, to the south of Winchester, which then completed the route to Southampton.

Whitchurch Station.

Throughout its life the railway was known by a couple of nicknames – the 'Desert Line', due to the fact that the line ran through large, unpopulated farming districts, and the 'Gold Coast Line' due to the colours of the surrounding countryside at harvest time. Newbury was the only major source of passengers on the route.

Sutton Scotney Station, 7 June 1919.

The 2.00 p.m. service from Newbury to Southampton at Worthy Down Halt, 4 September 1952.

King's Worthy Station.

King's Worthy Station, *c*.1909

London & South Western 4-4-0T, No. 321, at Winchester Chesil Station, November 1938.

Hayling Island Branch

Passenger service withdrawn	2 November 1963
Distance	4.5 miles (Havant to Hayling Island)
Company	Hayling Railway (1860–71)/ Brighton & South Coast Railway (1871–1923)

Stations closed	*Date*
Langston *	4 November 1963
North Hayling **	4 November 1963
Hayling Island ***	4 November 1963

Langston.

* Originally known as Langstone until May 1875; closed between December 1868 and August 1869.

** Closed between December 1868 and August 1869.

*** Closed in December 1868; renamed and reopened as South Hayling in August 1869; reverted to its original name on 1 June 1892.

Hayling Island Station.

Authorised in 1860 and opened in 1865, this line started from a bay platform at a busy main-line station and travelled over a large viaduct (which crossed the muddy waters of Langston Harbour) and along the exposed coastline of Hayling Island to the sandy beaches of its destination. There were four stations on the line. Havant was the connection with the main line and the start of the line. The Hayling Island trains had sole use of the bay platform there, as well as the watering and coaling facilities. Langstone was the first station (LBSCR dropped the 'E' from the name soon after taking control of the line) and the level crossing there caused traffic jams in the summer due to the busy train traffic. North Hayling, the second station, was located in a windswept and isolated position on the western edge of the island and there was a small siding there, used by the oyster trade in the harbour. Hayling Island, the terminus of the line, was located half a mile from the beach. The downfall of the line was the Langstone Viaduct, which was constructed using 1,100 feet of wooden trestles and there was a central swing bridge to allow small boats to pass through from Langstone to Chichester harbours. Until the commencement of the Second World War the signal box was manned to allow the bridge to be opened and closed. Even though the line was making a profit, the decaying viaduct meant that closure notices were posted at the end of 1962. The last timetabled service was on 2 November 1963 and was pulled by the oldest working locomotive then in operation on British Railways, No. 32636, with the Hayling Farewell Tour running the following day. Dismantling of the railway started in January 1967. To the locals of Hayling Island and Havant, the trains running on the line were affectionately known as 'Puffing Billys'.

Lee-on-the-Solent Light Railway

Passenger service withdrawn	31 December 1930
Distance	3 miles (Fort Brockhurst to Lee-on-the-Solent)
Company	Lee-on-the-Solent Light Railway (1893)/ London & South Western Railway (1893–1923)

Stations closed	*Date*
Fort Brockhurst *	31 December 1930
Fort Gomer **	1 May 1930
Browndown Halt ***	1 May 1930
Lee-on-the-Solent ***	1 January 1931

Browndown Halt, *c*.1908.

* This stood adjacent to Fort Brockhurst Station on the Bishopstoke to Gosport line.
** Originally known as Privett until October 1909; closed between 31 August and 1 October 1914.
*** Closed between 31 August and 1 October 1914.

Lee-on-the-Solent Station.

Authorised in 1893, the Lee-on-the-Solent Light Railway branched off the main line at Fort Brockhurst and travelled a little over 3 miles to its terminus adjacent to the pier at Lee. The railway itself was built on land acquired from the war department on a 99-year lease. There were three halts on the line: Privett (renamed as Fort Gomer Halt in order to avid confusion with a similarly named station on the Meon Valley Line), Browndown Halt and Elmore Halt, the latter of which was not opened until 11 April 1910. The line was quiet in comparison to some of the south coast lines, although traffic did increase during the First World War due to military construction work at Lee. In 1930 the line closed completely to passengers, the halts having closed on 1 May that year. Goods traffic continued for a further five years.

Mid Hants Railway

		Stations closed	Date
Passenger service withdrawn	February 1973	Itchen Abbas	5 February 1973
Distance	10 miles (Alton to Winchester via Alresford)		
Company	Alton, Alresford & Winchester Railway (1861–84)/ London & South Western Railway (1884–1923)		

Itchen Abbas Station.

Authorised in 1861 and opened in October 1865, the Alton, Alresford & Winchester Railway was a hilly alternative to the flat main track from London to Southampton. The line ran from Alton, where it joined the London & South Western Railway line to Guildford and London, to Winchester Junction (to the north of the city station) where it joined the London & South Western Railway main line from London to Southampton. The line was affectionately given two further names. The steam engine men called it 'Over the Alps' due to the need for such large engines to haul the freight. And, in the nineteenth century, farmers referred to the line as the 'Watercress Line' as it was used to rush their tender crops to consumers in London. The line closed to traffic in 1973. However, the section of the line between Alresford and Medstead was reopened in 1977 and became the Mid Hants Watercress Line – Hampshire's Heritage Railway. Besides Itchen Abbas, there were three other stations on the line – Medstead and Four Marks, Ropley, and Alresford and these three were all reopened as part of this enterprise.

Meon Valley Branch Railway

Passenger service withdrawn	5 February 1955
Distance	22.5 miles (Alton to Fareham via Droxford)
Company	London & South Western Railway

Stations closed	*Date*
Wickham	5 February 1955
Droxford	5 February 1955
West Meon	5 February 1955
Privett	5 February 1955
Tisted *	5 February 1955

* Known on some timetables as Tisted for Selbourne.

Wickham Station.

Droxford Station, *c*.1904.

This railway was built as the through route from London to Portsmouth via Alton and ran from Alton to Knowle Junction (two miles north of Fareham). Plans for the line began in 1851, however it was not authorised until 1897 and, although construction commenced the following year, it fell behind schedule and was not opened until 01 June 1903 – a year later than planned.

West Meon Station.

The line followed a picturesque route through thinly populated agricultural land and was constructed to main-line standards as a single track throughout, with room for a second track if needed. It had the unusual feature of having no terminus stations at either end; instead there were busy junctions (Fareham and Butts Junction).

A train from Fareham to Alton at Privett Station, 24 June 1949.

There were five main stations on the line, each with extensive buildings to include accommodation for the station masters, but it was unable to attract sufficient traffic and due to this only had a life span of 50 years. In 1944 a special train with the war cabinet on board stayed in a siding in Droxford in order to make the final preparations for the D-Day invasion of Normandy.

Northern & Southern Junction Railway (Hurstbourne to Fullerton Branch Railway) *

Passenger service withdrawn	6 July 1931
Distance	10 miles (Hurstbourne to Fullerton)
Company	London & South Western Railway (1863–1923)

Stations closed	*Date*
Longparish **	6 July 1931
Wherwell	6 July 1931

Longparish Station.

* This line was known by either of the names given here.

** Originally known as Long Parish, this was renamed on 1 July 1890.

Wherwell Station, 21 August 1965.

This double track line ran through the Harewood Forest and linked the London to Exeter line with the Andover to Redbridge line. The line came to be known as the 'Nile Valley' and this might have been because Queen Victoria likened the views from it to those of that location. Due to the fact that she disliked tunnels, this was her preferred route to the Isle of Wight. As a passenger line it was unsuccessful. In 1887 there were four weekday trains, but in 1914 this was reduced to four and then in 1920 to three. In 1913 the line was singled throughout and remained this way until closure in 1931. However, other uses were found for the line as there was an ammunition dump at Longparish during the Second World War (and the line at Wherwell had been used for the filming of the 1927 silent film, *The Ghost Train*). After the end of the war, the Longparish to Fullerton section was used as a test track for new rolling stock, although the line north of Longparish was completely closed on 29 May 1931.

Salisbury & Dorset Junction Railway *

Passenger service withdrawn	4 May 1964
Distance	19 miles (Salisbury to Poole via Fordingbridge)
Company	Salisbury & Dorset Junction Railway (1861–1883)/ London & South Western Railway (1883–1923)

Stations closed	*Date*
Breamore	4 May 1964
Fordingbridge	4 May 1964

Breamore Station, *c*.1912.

* Closed stations on this line that were in Wiltshire were Alderbury Road and Downton. The closed stations in Dorset were Daggons Road and Verwood.

Breamore Station.

In order to avoid a long detour via Southampton when travelling to Bournemouth and Poole, farmers and tradesman from the Salisbury area wanted a branch line built. Some landowners, along with the London & South Western Railway Company, initially opposed the building of the line but it eventually opened in 1866. It was 19 miles long and single track throughout, and saved 20 to 25 miles on a journey from Salisbury to Poole. Construction began on 3 February 1864, when a 'cheery crowd saw Countess Nelson from nearby Trafalgar House at Downton, Wiltshire, cut the first sod'. The actual route ran from Alderbury Junction to West Moors on the Brockenhurst to Wimbourne line and was the second line to be built in the New Forest.

Fordingbridge Station, *c*.1902.

The London & South Western Railway Company continued to make life difficult, but eventually their obstructive ways paid off and they bought the line in 1883. They continued to treat it with contempt, even though it had a good excursion trade to Bournemouth and on several occasions brought upwards of 3,000 people to enjoy the festivals held at the Moot in Downton.

The winter timetable for 1900/01 was as inconvenient as possible, with only six trains each way every day. The 1901 summer timetable was only slightly better, this time with seven trains each way.

Fordingbridge after closure, 22 August 1965.

Stokes Bay Branch

Passenger service withdrawn	1 November 1915
Distance	2 miles (Gosport to Stokes Bay)
Company	Stokes Bay Railway & Pier Company (1855–75)/ London & South Western Railway (1875–1922)

Stations closed	*Date*
Gosport Road & Alverstoke *	1 November 1915
Stokes Bay	1 November 1915

* Originally known as Stoke Road and renamed Gosport Road on 8 November 1866. Renamed again in October 1893.

On 14 August 1855 the Stokes Bay & Isle of Wight Pier Company was authorised to build a railway. Their view was to provide an easy link to the Isle of Wight from Stokes Bay, the closest point to the island on the south coast mainland and this opened on 6 April 1863. The idea was a good one, but passengers were inconvenienced by having to travel into Gosport and then out again to Stokes Bay. The construction of the triangle north of Gosport Station removed this problem by allowing direct access to the pier via Stoke Road Station (later known as Gosport Road). The London & South Western Railway took over the branch in 1875 and that year they provided a two and three-quarter hour service from London Waterloo to Ryde on the Isle of Wight. This was half an hour faster than could have been achieved via Portsmouth, but the service was short lived due to the opening of Portsmouth Harbour Station the following year. This station provided an alternative route to the Isle of Wight and did not suffer from services being halted due to bad weather, as could happen at Stokes Bay. The steamer service from the bay was withdrawn in 1913 and passenger services ceased in 1915. During the First World War the line and Stokes Bay pier were used to transport military goods and in 1922 the Admiralty purchased the pier, for a short time using it for stock storage. However, by the late 1930s the railway track had been lifted.

Southsea Railway

		Stations closed	Date
Passenger service withdrawn	8 August 1914	Jessie Road Bridge Halt	6 August 1914
Distance	1.25 miles (Fratton to Southsea)	East Southsea	8 August 1914
Company	Southsea Railway Company (1885–86)/ London & South Western Railway and London, Brighton & South Coast Railway (1886–1914)		

Authorised in 1880, this line was built to serve Victorian holidaymakers travelling to the seaside and the steamers bound for the Isle of Wight. Construction began in 1884 and the double-track line opened on 1 July the following year. In 1886 the railway was sold to a joint committee of the London & South Western Railway and the London, Brighton & South Coast Railway and an agreement was put in place that they would operate the line on alternate years. There were only two stations on the line, Fratton (still open) and Southsea. The terminus station at Southsea was located in Granada Road. The station was of Queen Anne style and consisted of three platforms, each being 360ft in length. To help attract more customers, the owners of the railway opened two further halts in Southsea on 1 October 1904, one at Highland Road and the other at Jessie Road Bridge. The final train ran on 8 August 1914. During the First World War the line was used for military storage, with the expectancy of reopening after the war. However, this did not happen and confirmation of closure was issued in 1919. The track was torn up and its bridges were demolished in 1923.

Swindon, Grayton & Marlborough Railway *

		Stations closed	Date
Passenger service withdrawn	11 September 1961	Weyhill	11 September 1961
Distance	59.5 miles (in total)		
Company	Swindon, Grayton & Marlborough Railway (1873–1944)/ Midland & South Western Junction Railway (1844–1923)		

* The closed stations on this line that were in Wiltshire were Ludgershall, Collingbourne Kingston Halt, Collingbourne, Grafton & Burbage, Savernake High Level, Marlborough Low Level, Ogbourne, Chiseldon Camp Halt, Chiseldon, Swindon Town, Rushey Platt, Moredon Platform, Blunsdon, and Cricklade. The closed stations that were in Gloucestershire were Cerney, Ashton Keyes, Cirencester, Foss Cross, Chedworth Halt, Withington, and Andoversford & Dowdeswell.

Weyhill was the southernmost station on the Swindon, Grayton & Marlborough Railway and the only one on the line that was in Hampshire. As with other stations of the era, it was situated some distance from the village it was built to serve. Weyhill was famous for its annual fair, held in October, and this was an extremely valuable source of traffic for the railway.

Totton, Hythe & Fawley Light Railway

Passenger service withdrawn	14 February 1966
Distance	9.5 miles (Totton to Fawley)
Company	Totton, Hythe & Fawley Light Railway (1921–23)

Stations closed	*Date*
Marchwood	14 February 1966
Hythe (Hants)	14 February 1966
Fawley	14 February 1966

The first passenger train arrives at Fawley Station, 1925.

In 1921 the Totton, Hythe & Fawley Light Railway Company was formed with the sole purpose of building a standard gauge railway along the edge of Southampton Water from Totton to Fawley. On 20 July 1925 the line was opened, almost 20 years after the first plans had been laid down. The line followed an easy, picturesque route along the wooded west bank of Southampton Water and journeyed through the villages of Marchwood and Hythe before reaching its terminus at Fawley. At Marchwood there was a connection on the down side of the line which gave access to the military port there. As the country branch line era ended, the railway failed to attract a significant amount of traffic and this should have meant early closure for the line. However, due to the oil refinery at Fawley it remained in use. On 3 March 1958 a new halt was opened to serve the village of Hardley, this halt was never advertised and closed in April 1965, only seven years after opening. The last passenger train ran on Saturday 12 February 1966, with the official stoppage of passenger services taking place on Monday 14 February 1966. Although the passenger services ceased, the freight services continued and still run today on what has become a busy freight route.

Closed stations on lines still open to passengers

Line/Service		*Stations closed*	*Date*
	Basingstoke & Salisbury Railway	Oakley	17 June 1963
		Hurstbourne	6 June 1964

Oakley Station.

Hurstbourne Station.